LETTS ❖ PATTERN ❖ LIBRARY

CHRISTMAS
❖ PATTERNS ❖

CHARLES LETTS

Letts®

FOUNDED 1796

Designed and edited by
Anness Publishing Ltd
4a The Old Forge
7 Caledonian Road
London N1 9DX

First published 1991
by Charles Letts & Co Ltd
Diary House, Borough Road
London SE1 1DW

British Library Cataloguing in Publication Data
Christmas patterns. – (Letts pattern library)
1.   Decorative arts. Special subjects. Christmas
I.   Title
745

ISBN 1-85238–125–6

"Letts" is a registered trademark of
Charles Letts (Scotland) Ltd.

Editorial Director: Joanna Lorenz
Designer: Mike Snell
Illustrator: Janos Marffy

Printed and bound in Great Britain by
Butler & Tanner Ltd, Frome and London

CONTENTS

INTRODUCTION   4

FATHER CHRISTMAS   8

NATIVITY   10

SNOWMEN   16

ANIMALS   18

DECORATIONS   24

CANDLES AND CENTREPIECES   28

FLOWERS   32

CHILDREN   38

TRADITIONAL CHRISTMAS   42

INTRODUCTION

For many of us Christmas is the most important and exciting festival season of the year – a time when people all around the world simultaneously break off from their everyday activities to celebrate. This book of Christmas patterns and designs has been created to add new dimensions to the festivities by providing you with hundreds of ideas for extra flourishes that can be applied to everything from cards, decorations and gift-wrapping to cakes, table-linen and children's Christmas stockings.

To make it easier to find a particular design the book is broken down into simple sections: Father Christmas, Candles and Centrepieces, Traditional Christmas, Snowmen, Nativity, Animals, Children, Decorations and Flowers. Don't be afraid to mix and match among the various sections to create your own effects, and remember that the individual ideas included can also be integrated into larger designs such as borders, motifs, repeat patterns or set pieces (such as a complete nativity scene) in your own style.

The patterns in this book can be used in myriad ways. The following are just a few of the possible techniques and crafts for which they are suitable: stencilling, collage, block-printing, fabric painting, ceramic painting, painting onto wooden toys, crewel work, embroidery, appliqué work, quilling, watercolour and oil painting, cut-out work and so on. The patterns can be adapted for knitting or quilting, and they can also be used in sugarcraft, for buttercream and frosting designs, moulded flowers, novelty cakes, lace and filigree designs, and jelly and wafer painting.

Objects which can be decorated include virtually anything which plays a part in the festival season – these are just a few ideas: Christmas cakes (and mince pies!), Christmas-tree decorations, gift-wrappings, table-linen and table-ware, Christmas cards, party invitations, Christmas decorations, table-centres, gift tags, toys and Christmas stockings. Even clothes and bed-linen can be decorated: nothing highlights the excitement of Christmas as much for a small child as a Father Christmas pillow-slip or snowman scarf and hat to be used on only a few special days a year.

ADAPTING THE PATTERNS

Use your own creative skills and your imagination. The patterns have all been drawn in a very simple way, with no shading or fine inner line work, so that they are as easy as possible to use, and they allow the flexibility for you to add your own personal touches. Bear in mind that some of the patterns are life-size but that others are smaller; you may decide, in any case, to use them at various different sizes to fit a particular area of your work. Remember, too, that you can flip the patterns over using different techniques to give a mirror image of the design.

The designs can be used individually, or a combination can be made into a tableau or repeat pattern. The easiest way to do this is to draw the chosen piece on tracing paper then place the designs on top of each other and move them until you are happy with the arrangement. Finally trace the whole thing and transfer it onto the required surface.

If you want to use the pattern at the same size you can simply trace the outline onto tracing paper, but if the design you want to use is too large or too small, you can enlarge or reduce it in two ways. One simple way is to use a photocopier with an enlarging and reducing mode, which will ensure that the design is faithfully reproduced; just copy the image to the size required. However, most machines only enlarge up to 156% of the original size, so you would have to use the machine twice if you wanted to double the size of the design. This method also depends of course on your having access to a photocopier with this facility, although an increasing number of shops now offer a photocopying service.

The other, traditional, method is to draw the image to a different size by hand, using the grid method. This is not difficult for most designs, although accuracy is important and you may have problems if the design is very intricate. The technique consists of drawing a grid of squares over the original design and then copying the design, square for square, onto a larger (or smaller, if you want to reduce the size) grid. In this book the designs are all drawn with ready-made grid lines, so that they can be transferred simply to another sheet of paper to an increased or reduced size.

USING THE PATTERNS AS TEMPLATES

You can also use the patterns to make templates for cutting and drawing around. Trace the design onto tracing paper then onto thin plastic, for instance the top of a plastic ice cream container. Cut the shape out and you will have a very strong, durable template. Cardboard, oiled parchment and clear acetate are other good materials, which can be used again and again, even on moist surfaces. You could, for instance, make holly leaf and berry

The Grid Method

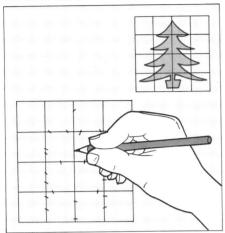 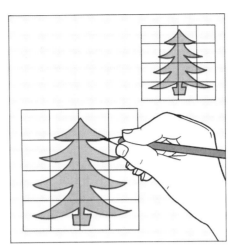 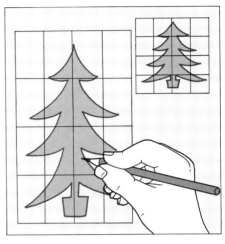

On a piece of paper, draw up an area of the size you want the finished image to be – larger or smaller depending on whether you want to enlarge or reduce the design. Fill with grid squares matching the pattern of those that surround the original drawing; the important thing is to have the same number of squares on both grid patterns. Now copy the original square by square onto the second version, marking the points at which the original design bisects a line on the new grid.

Follow the points as a guide to where your pen should go. Always check the copied design against the original, and draw over the lines to make sure that they are fluid and continuous.

A variation of this technique is to use it to change the proportions by distorting the original design. For example, to have a design that fits a long, sleek shape, you might decide that the drawing would look best if made thinner. So, draw up a second grid that corresponds in position to the original, but with vertical rectangles instead of squares.

Cutting Stencils

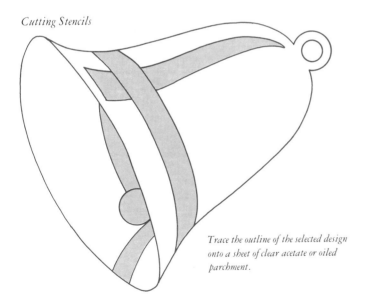

Trace the outline of the selected design onto a sheet of clear acetate or oiled parchment.

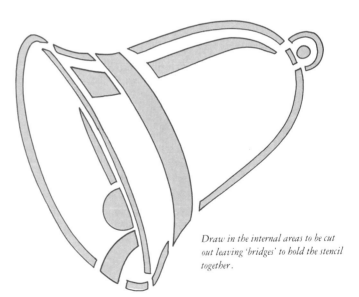

Draw in the internal areas to be cut out leaving 'bridges' to hold the stencil together.

designs in flower (gum) paste or marzipan. Another idea is to cut the leaves and berries out of pastry to fashion tiny holly sprigs on mince pies (these can be painted with green and red edible dyes).

USING THE PATTERNS AS STENCILS

A stencil is a very useful way of making a re-usable pattern to repeat shapes onto a variety of surfaces, including paper and card, fabric, ceramics, wood, and sugarpaste (or fondant) covered cakes. To make a stencil pattern from the designs in this book, trace the outline onto clear acetate or oiled parchment, and carefully cut it away on the inside using a sharp craft knife. When doing this, remember to build in 'bridges' over the internal lines that divide the main parts of the design, or where you want a change of colour. Beware when cutting a dense or complicated design as much of its main body will be cut away, making it very weak. The bridge-like links should come at regular intervals to hold the stencil together. If you want to avoid using bridges, you will need to cut a separate stencil for each area of colour and apply one after the other, allowing the paint to dry in between.

A stencil pattern can be used directly onto fabrics (specially designed water-based paints are available, which are 'set' with a hairdryer or by pressing when dry with a hot iron. They are also attractive on walls and make lovely friezes and borders around doorways, ceilings and pictures; a variety of acrylic, emulsion (latex) and oil-based paints are available, and stencil crayons and spray paints can also be used. You may not want Christmas patterns on the walls all year round but by applying your frieze to card or good-quality, well-crafted paper it can be put up during the festival period with the rest of the decorations, and then packed carefully into storage for the following year. An alternative is to make a stencilled Christmas screen (perhaps to frame the back of your Christmas tree) which, again, can be stored from year to year. Wood dyes and stains give a pretty stencilled effect on wooden surfaces, and this technique can also be used for Christmas table-centres, brightly coloured Christmas-tree decorations, or even a lovely wooden Christmas toy box which only comes out once a year.

When using a stencil, attach it firmly around the edges on the required surface and blot in the colour. Be sure to use edible dusting powders on sugarpaste, but for most decorative purposes you can use standard eggshell or emulsion paint, signwriter's paint, acrylic artist's paint and even car spray paint (which should be applied only in a well-ventilated room).

TRANSFERRING THE PATTERNS ONTO FABRIC

To transfer a design onto fabric for embroidery or painting with fabric paint, first trace the desired drawing on tracing paper to the required size. Place on the fabric and insert pins through the paper around the outline and along the inner line work. Tear the paper away and mark the line of the pins with dressmaker's chalk.

Another method is to place a sheet of dressmaker's carbon paper between the traced design and the fabric; go over the pattern again with a sharp instrument or pencil. The carbon lines will transfer to the fabric, and can then be reinforced with dressmaker's chalk or a fabric marking pen. The carbon washes out.

Alternatively, use water-soluble fabric marking pens, tracing the design onto tracing paper and then onto the fabric. If it is thin enough to see through simply lay the fabric directly over the design and trace (place the design under the fabric on a special light box or against a window, and draw directly onto the material). After the outline has been filled in or embroidered over as required, the pen marks can be washed out in cold water. Fade-out marker pens, too, can be used – the lines do not require washing out but simply fade away. A variety of dressmaker's tracing pencils are also available.

TRANSFERRING THE PATTERNS ONTO OTHER OBJECTS

Carbon paper can be used to transfer the designs onto 3-dimensional objects, such as pots, Christmas-tree balls, table-ware, or wood, which can then be painted or drawn over in your chosen style. Trace the design accurately onto a piece of tracing paper cut to a size so that there is a generous margin around the design. Cut a piece of carbon paper to roughly the same size, and position it, carbon-side down, on the area of the object onto which you want to transfer the design. Place the piece of tracing paper on top of the carbon paper, and stick it temporarily in place with a small piece of masking tape (this ensures that the paper does not slip while you are transferring the design). Now draw over the traced lines of the design, pressing hard with the tip of a pencil so that the carbon paper transfers the motif onto the surface. By moving it, you can use the same piece of carbon paper many times.

TRANSFERRING THE PATTERNS ONTO ICED CAKES

Once you have chosen the design, trace it onto tracing paper and then transfer it onto your royal icing- or fondant-covered cake or plaque surface, making sure the surface is dry and firm. Transferring is best done with a stylus, a metal tool with a minute ball on the end, which is used by placing the pattern onto the required surface and gliding the stylus like a pencil over the design to transfer it. You can then pipe over the embedded outline in icing. A more traditional method is to prick holes through the tracing paper into the surface.

When transferring onto a soft or semi-soft surface, use either a copy projector, which illuminates the design using light reflex onto the cake surface (then pipe or paint directly onto the lines shown), or first pipe the design onto a piece of clear plastic such as perspex or plexiglass, using royal icing made without glycerine. Let this dry and then press the piped design gently but firmly onto the required surface; lift off carefully to reveal an embossed, mirror image outline. Royal icing can be used a few times in this way; if you want to make a permanent embosser, you could pipe the design using a flexible bathroom or kitchen tile sealer rather than icing. This, once dry, can be used many times.

Using the Patterns for Buttercream and Frosting Work
Trace your required image or combination of designs with a black pen onto tracing paper or cellophane, plexiglass or clear plastic, then, using a copy projector, project the design onto the buttercream-covered cake surface. Pipe over the design with buttercream in a colour of your choice and allow to dry; the inner areas can then be filled with piped buttercream, piping jelly or melted chocolate (candy).

An alternative method is to pipe the design in melted chocolate (candy) onto a piece of glass, perspex or plexiglass, and once set press onto the buttercream-covered cake surface. Pipe over this embossed image with buttercream of a different colour. Remember that by using this method you will get a reverse image.

Another way is to mark an area onto waxed paper to represent the size of the cake, and pipe the design onto it. Fill in with buttercream, using a different colour for the design in the middle. For example, if your cake is 25cm (10″) you would have a 25cm (10″) circle of buttercream on waxed paper, with the image area of the design filled in the middle. Pipe the buttercream so that it is about 1cm (½″) thick. Then put another piece of waxed paper on top and place in the deep freezer until solid. Pull the top layer off, flip it over onto the cake surface and pull off the bottom layer of waxed paper to reveal the flat, smooth pattern.

Using the Patterns for Sugarcraft Piping
To pipe images in either royal icing or buttercream, trace the basic design onto tracing paper, cut this out and stick it onto the top of a nail or cake pick. Place waxed paper squares over this and pipe on the extra detail or devices. This ensures identical reproduction, with perfect results every time.

Using the Patterns for Sugarcraft Lace and Filigree Work
Pipe over the basic outline onto waxed paper using a no.0 or no.1 nozzle/tube/tip, then fill in the design freehand using small joined-up S and C scrolls, or a fish scale design. (This inside work would be piped with a no.0 or no.00 nozzle.) The pieces can be slid off the paper when dry.

Using the Patterns for Sugarcraft Jelly and Wafer Painting
This is a very quick and easy way to place a design onto your cake. Using a piece of rice/wafer paper, trace on the design using a paintbrush and food colouring or melted chocolate (candy), or an edible food colour pen, then stick this face-up directly onto your cake surface. This will be no problem on buttercream, but with sugarpaste (rolled fondant) first lightly steam the surface with a kettle, let it dry a little so that it is just sticky, and then press the design onto the cake surface. Because the rice/wafer paper is absorbed into the cake surface, you will just be left with your chosen design.

SOME SUGGESTED FURTHER USES FOR THE PATTERNS

3-Dimensional Effects
The designs can also be used for making up 3-dimensional objects in silk, paper, fabric and sugarpaste. The floral patterns are particularly suitable for this technique, and the results can even be made into sprays or arrangements by combining various elements together. Trace off the components of the design separately and make into individual templates in cardboard or thin plastic. Place over your desired surface and cut out around the templates with scissors, scalpel or modelling knife. Form or shape as required – you may want to 'build up' some of the elements by using thicker card, fabric, or sugarpaste to add depth – then assemble the pieces together to create a 3-dimensional arrangement.

Another method is to cut out 2 or 3 identical designs, paint them and then place them in layers directly above each other with spacers in between.

Crewel Work
Once the design has been transferred onto the fabric or cake, lines are then embroidered or piped in to fill the area. When doing this, draw the lines just as if you were writing with a pen, so that the lines sit evenly and fill in all of the design area.

Appliqué Work
Trace out the component elements of the design and use these to make plastic or cardboard templates. With the templates, cut the shapes out of fabric, paper, sugarpaste (rolled fondant) or other material, and place them onto the required surface. Once in place, very fine stitches are usually sewn, painted or piped around the edge.

Cut-Out Work
The designs can be adapted for cut-work embroidery, if a simple pattern is chosen. Trace the design onto the fabric, usually firm linen or cotton, cutting out areas as required, but leaving enough 'bridges' so that the holes are not too large or fragile – much the same procedure as cutting out a stencil. The strengthening bars and outlines can then be embroidered in a colour to match the fabric.

Quilling
This 3-dimensional technique is essentially a paper craft but can also be adapted for sugarcraft using long thin strips of paste. Once the basic outline is taken from the book, transfer it onto the required surface (see techniques described earlier), draw, paint or pipe on the outline, then roll up and insert the strips. (For sugarpaste (rolled fondant) strips, a quick tip is to use a hero cutter or a rotary cutter, or even a tagliatelle maker on an electric pasta machine.)

FATHER CHRISTMAS

Jolly Santas

Father Christmas on the roof

Riding over the rooftops with Rudolph

Santas

NATIVITY

The three Kings

Three Kings, Mary, Joseph and Jesus

Shepherds

Paying homage to the baby

Animals by the crib

The three Kings approach

Angels

The star over Bethlehem

Mary and Jesus at the manger

The Christmas star

Madonna and Child

Angels

Choirboy

The angel Gabriel

The Christmas star

Welcoming baby Jesus

Minstrels

SNOWMEN

Tobogonning

Snowman with scarf

Peeping at the decorations

Snowman with carrot nose

Snowball fights

Animals

Peace dove

Reindeer

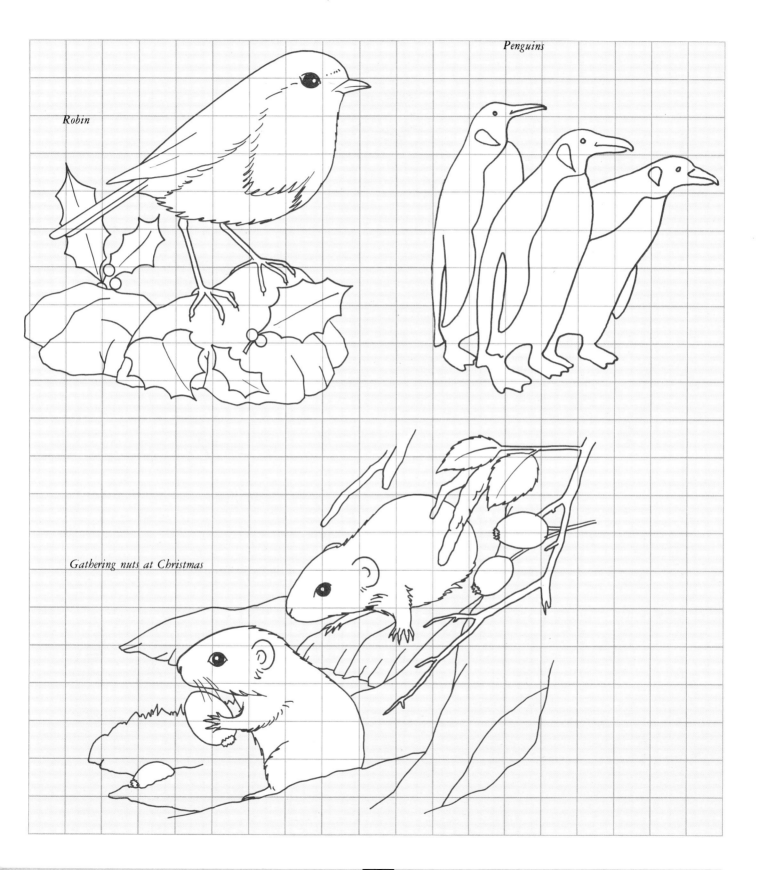

Robin

Penguins

Gathering nuts at Christmas

Gathering food in the snow

Robin and snowdrops

Dove

Robin

Rabbits in the snow

Waiting for spring

Owl at the church window

Robin red-breast

Robins in winter

Pheasant and snowy trees

DECORATIONS

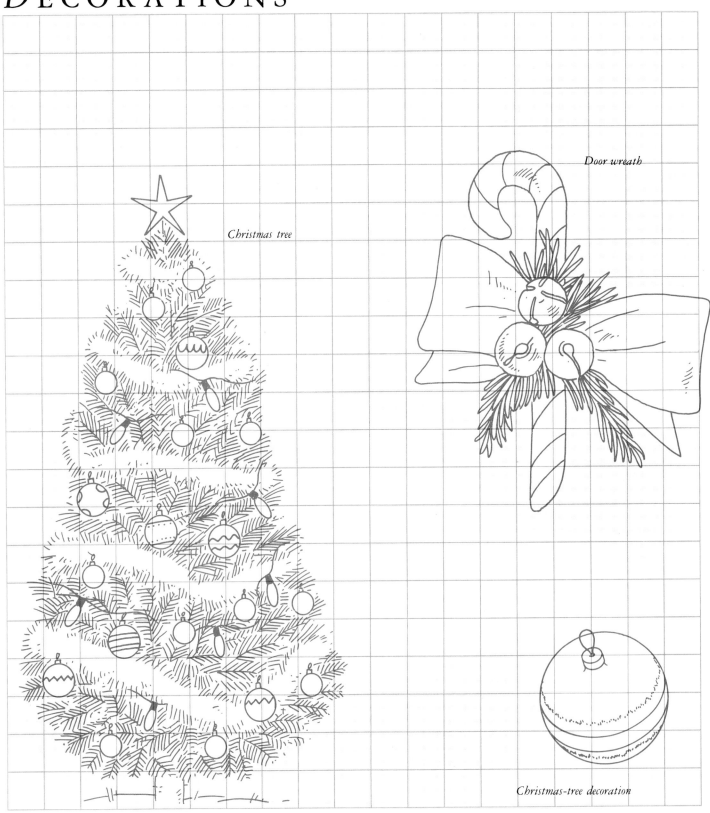

Christmas tree

Door wreath

Christmas-tree decoration

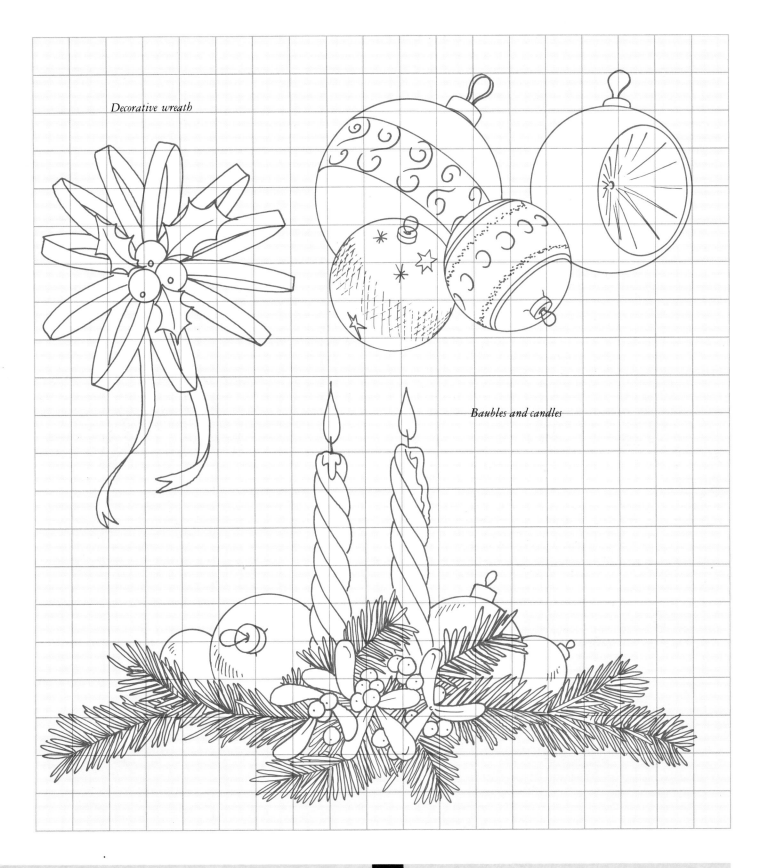

Decorative wreath

Baubles and candles

Seasonal messages

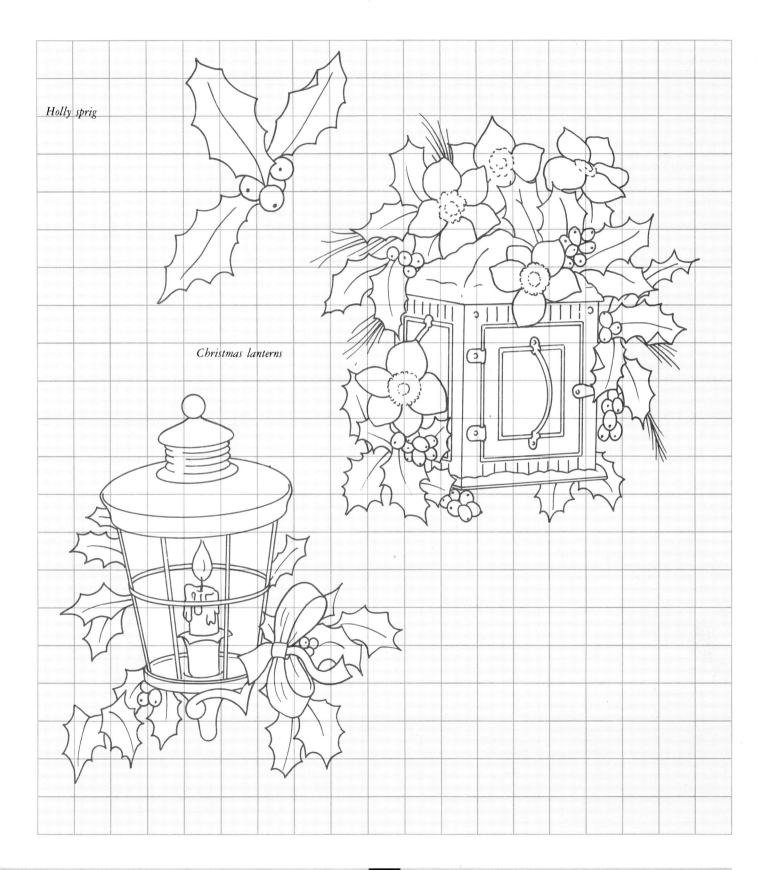

Holly sprig

Christmas lanterns

CANDLES AND CENTREPIECES

Baubles

Fruit for Christmas day

Snowman candle

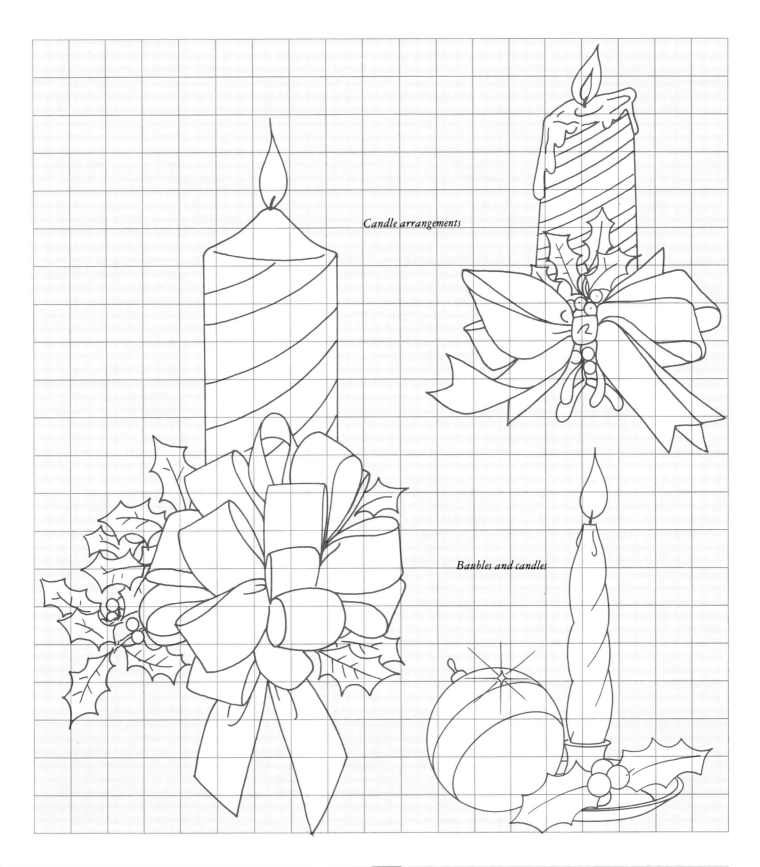

Candle arrangements

Baubles and candles

Decorative candle

Winter arrangement

Candles

FLOWERS

Arrangements in containers

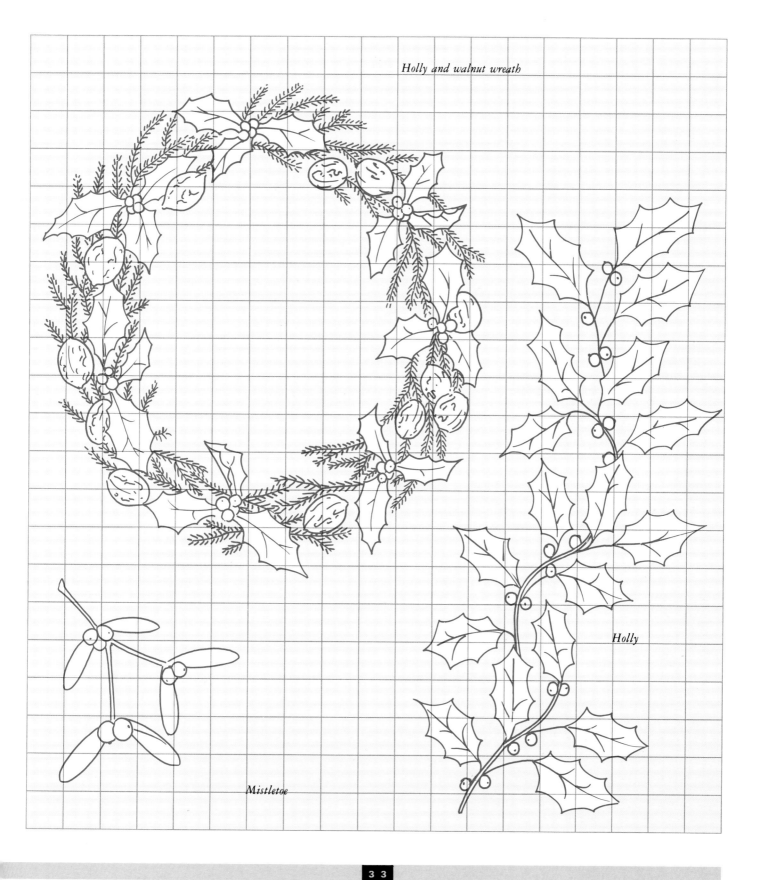

Holly and walnut wreath

Holly

Mistletoe

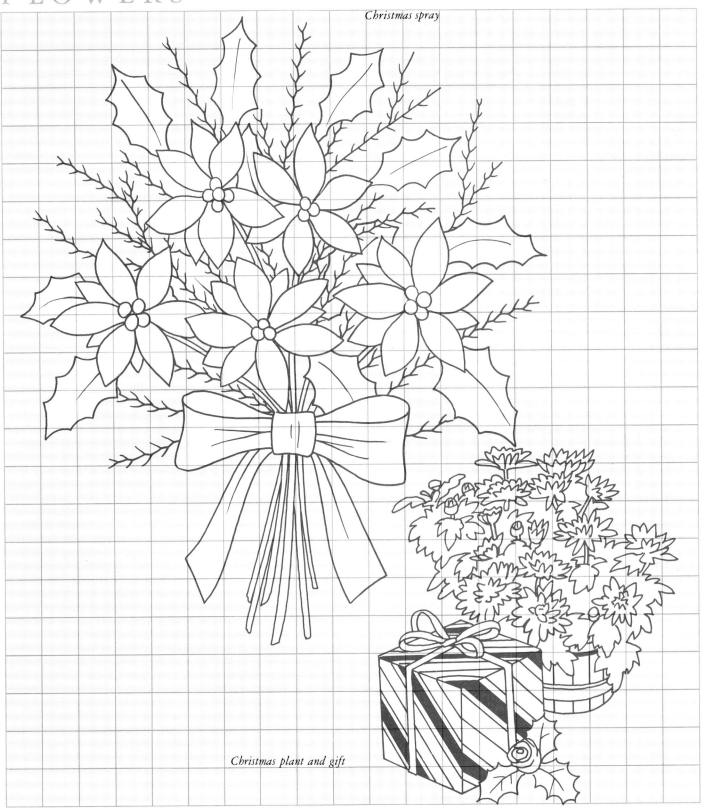

Christmas spray

Christmas plant and gift

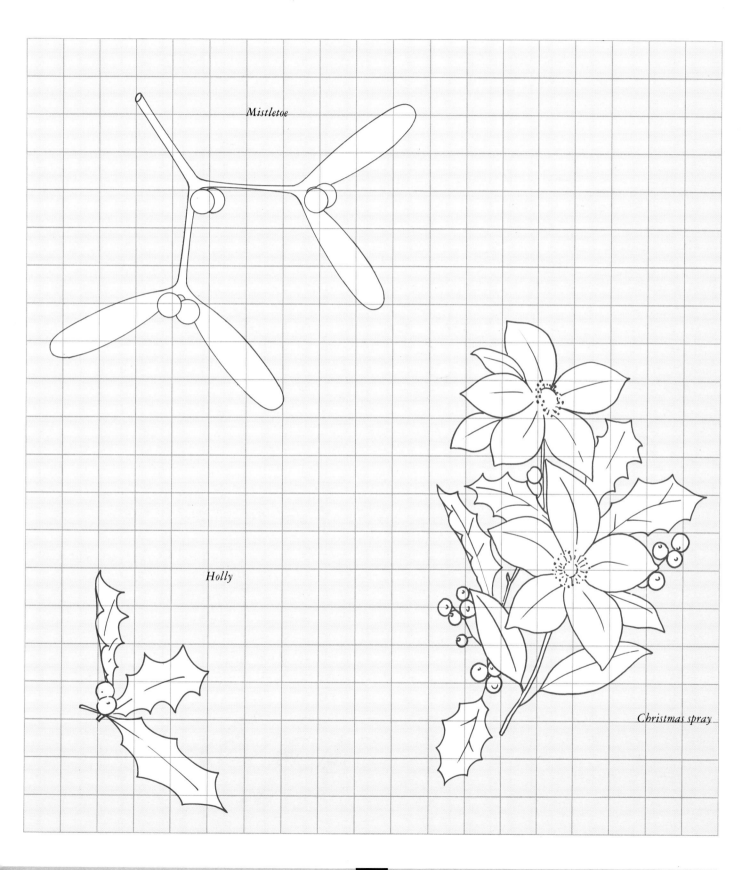

Mistletoe

Holly

Christmas spray

FLOWERS

Poinsettia with festive candles

Poinsettia blooms

Mistletoe

Christmas rose

Christmas arrangement

CHILDREN

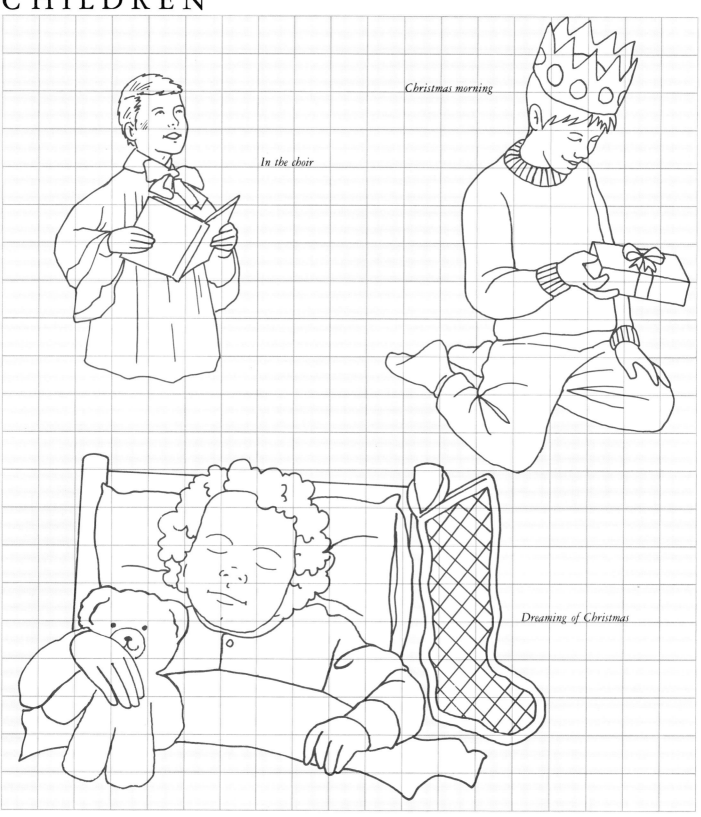

In the choir

Christmas morning

Dreaming of Christmas

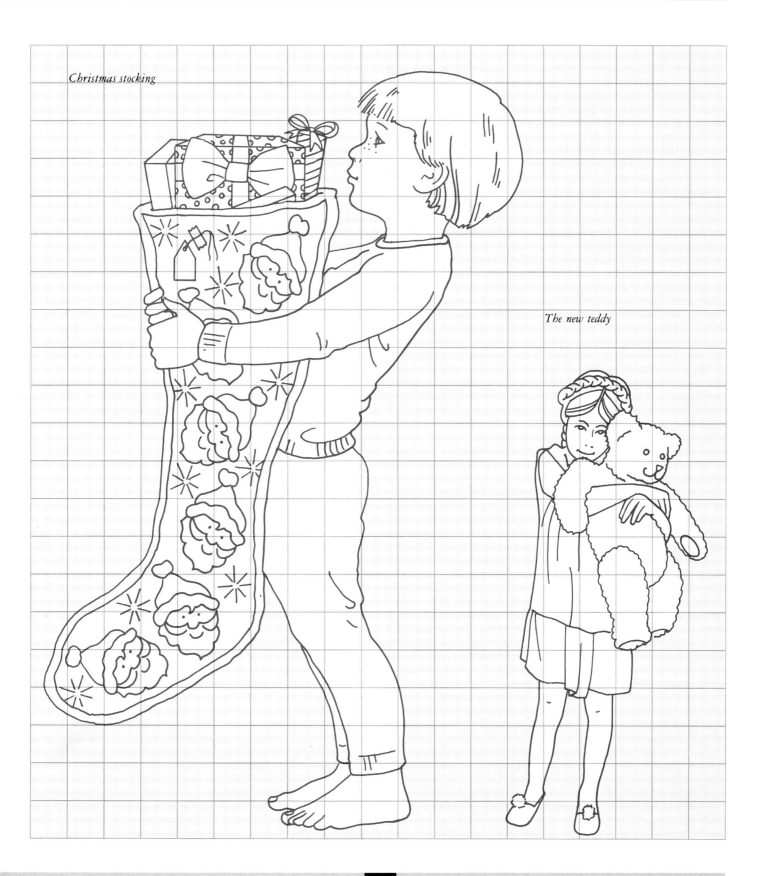

Christmas stocking

The new teddy

Playing with presents

Building a snowman

Carol singers

Christmas fun

TRADITIONAL CHRISTMAS

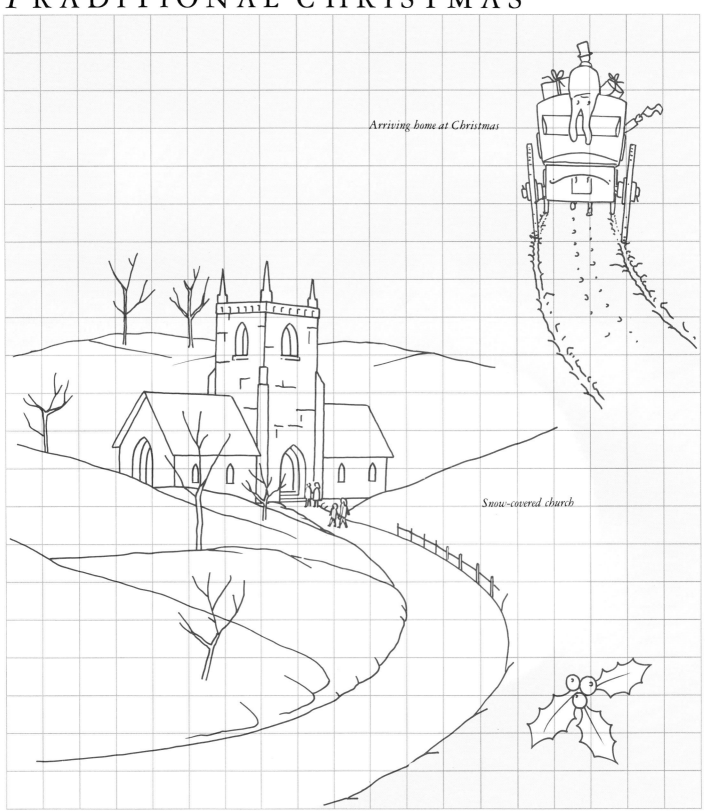

Arriving home at Christmas

Snow-covered church

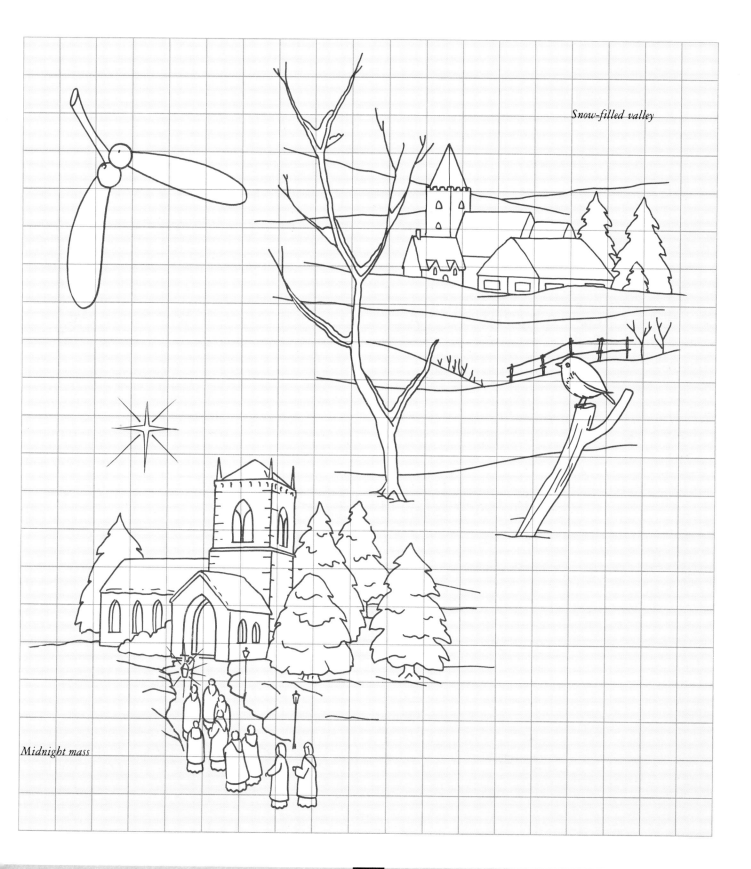

Snow-filled valley

Midnight mass

Visiting Santa's grotto

Christmas stocking

Victorian plum pudding

"A merry Christmas, Ma'am!"

Christmas-tree fairy

Gathering holly

Peace at Christmas

Special toys

Christmas turkey

Christmas pudding

Snow on the bridge

The Christmas visit

Roasting chestnuts

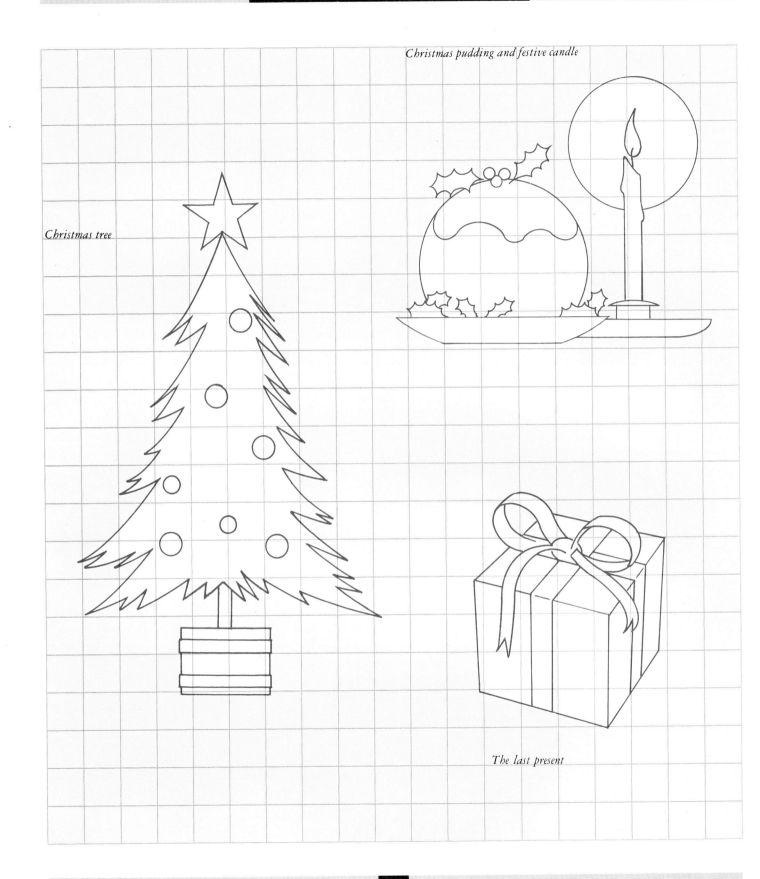

Christmas pudding and festive candle

Christmas tree

The last present